D0996897

# The Poet Cat

# The Poet Cat

## Poems by Grace Nichols

### Illustrated by Bee Willey

BLOOMSBURY
CHILDREN'S
BOOKS

First published in Great Britain in 2000
Bloomsbury Publishing Plc, 38 Soho Square, London, W1V 5DF

ISBN 0 7475 5064 6

Printed in Great Britain by Clays Ltd, St Ives plc

10 9 8 7 6 5 4 3 2 1

*To Kalera and all cat-folk,*
*and to Yansan who was there*
*for the feline coming*

# Contents

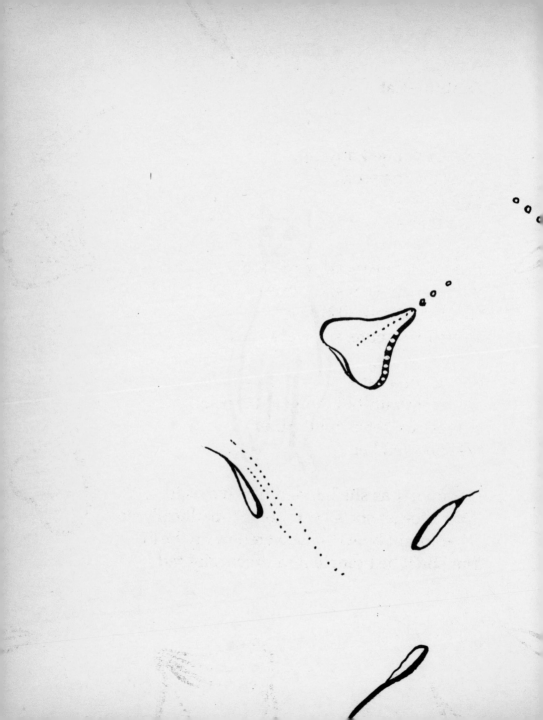

## Drat-the-Cat

I never wanted any cat,
all that extra work
I thought –
Drat that –

But my six-year-old made me
with her six-year-old pleas –
Please O Please O Please
so small, so cute, so sweet.

So we got a cat –
a three-month-old tabby to be exact,
scattery as petals on the day
we collected her.

Her owner as she handed her over said,
'Don't forget she's been homoeopathically bred,'
'That might be so,' I answered in my head,
'but she'll be homely and practically fed.'

# The Naming

Even with a cat-dictionary
we couldn't for the life of me
decide on a name for the cat.

Clarissa? Too aristocrat
Marmalade? Too smoothie
Cocoa? Too sleepy
Willow? Too weepy
Primrose? Too prim
Cassandra? Too grim
Minnie? Too neat
Lavender? Too sweet.

Then my daughter spotted her asleep on
my half-open Roget's *Thesaurus*
and squealed out just like that,

'Let's call her Thesaura,
it suits her cat-character,
and besides, she is a girl-cat.'

Thesaura, Thesaura,
if ever there was a cat
that made a book into a sofa,
that cat is Thesaura.

## Who?

Who is that
small stripy
grey and black
hurricane
flashing about
the house like
           lightning

Coming in slow motion
across the kitchen

Circling my ankles
cyclonically

Brushing me
like a velvet wind

Making me
the centre of her storm.

15

## Red Alert

Red alert, red alert,
there's a cat among my poems.

Repeat cat
among poems in progress

CAT –
small feline

Claws, paws, fur,
that kind of thing

Whiskers, sticky-up ears,
mean anything?

Maiow, Maiow,
still no bells ringing?

Purr, purr,
scratch, scratch

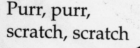

Distant cousin
to jungle's big cats.

Retired from jungle to house
with humans – never looked back

Finds goldfish fascinating,
likes a good stroke in lap.

In Russia, *Koskha*,
In France, *le Chat*.

In Romania, *Pisicca*,
In English plain Cat.

Still don't get it?
Ah forget it.

Roger-Roger over out.

17

## The First Cat

How did she come, the first cat,
to the first home,
all those thousands
and thousands of years ago?

Did she come hunger-driven
and flea-bitten,
scratching with a whine
at the door of humankind?

Did she come all glum
seeking political asylum,
chased from her jungle home
by bigger animals on the roam?

Did she come sneaky
as a shadow
slipping through
some left-open window?

Did she come with style,
did she come with grace,
did she come bold-face
with eyes that seem to say,

'Look, in exchange for being a houser,
I will become a mouser
of the first order –
can't say better than that.'

How did she come – the first cat?

## Strength to Strength

It's difficult to keep a cat
at arm's length –
so she grows from strength to strength,
taking up all your best places for herself,
like the warm cosy chair you've just left.

The genuine puzzlement on her face
as she boldly yet soulfully
meets your gaze, tells you
she is truly amazed
that you should object in any way.

And with a look of lofty reproachment
she settles down on your pillow with its
lavender scent, in utter utter feline contentment.

## Brainy

She's brainy
she's literary

Head resting on my
*English Dictionary*

Belly on my
*Treasury of Poetry*

Rump plum on my
*Classic Fairy Tales*

Tail encircling *The Complete Works of Shakespeare*

Paw gentle on my old typewriter

As if she's secretly dreaming

Of pawing into print a poetic bestseller.

# A Small Tiger

I never forget she's a small tiger,
her slanting eyes are a great reminder,
the way she pounces and swishes her tail
   about her,
I never forget she's a small tiger.

We go into the back garden when we can't
   find her,
There she is – trying to claw-catch
One of the birds flying above her,
I never forget she's a small tiger.

Sometimes she stays out all night,
I can only lie in bed and wonder,
What she's up to, this midnight prowler?
I never forget she's a small tiger.

Sitting there looking all queen-like and clever
With her curling tail and her eyes of amber,
But when I'm not feeling well, this small tiger
comes and inspects me like a concerned doctor.

Her medicine is her purr which makes me
    much better.
My small tiger – I'm so glad to have her.

## Accordion

When I tell my daughter off
about squeezing the cat, she says,

I'm not squeezing the cat
we're performing a musical double-act

The cat is my accordion
when I press her to my heart
I am playing Mozart.

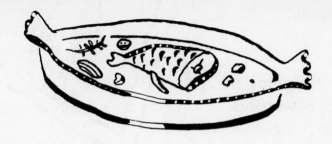

## Attitude Problem

She's a cat with at—
that's attitude,
won't accept no platitude,
won't even sniff at my leftover fishstew,
just looks at me coldly
as if to say, 'One is not amused.'
That's what you get for gratitude,
when you give a cat too much latitude –
a haughty heap of cattitude.

## Cat-Shots

1.  Sitting upright
    with her legs
    well together –
    a beautiful vase
    that doesn't need
    a flower.

2.  Lying on the fish-tank
    like the Guardian of Fish,
    looking so benevolent
    but there's a deep fish-wish.

3.  Standing by the door
    like a real little muggins,
    wanting to stay out
    yet wanting to come in.

4. Soaking up all the sunshine
   on that patch there –
   a cyclist who likes to be
   tickled on her back
   while she pedals the air.

5. Behind the curtains
   on the window-sill,
   an actress pacing
   just before the show begins.

# When the Cat Ignores My Daughter, She Says . . .

Mum, I don't think the cat
likes me anymore
she use to run behind me
when I run through the door

She use to run behind me
down the passageway
like a cheetah
but not any longer

She use to be a playing-cat
a pawing-cat
a pouncy
bring-my-ball-of-paper back cat

She use to be a daring-cat
a scaring-cat
a pretend to
bite-my-toes kind of cat

Now all she wants to do
is sit and stare
as if she's trying to bring
something out of the air.

It isn't fair.

## What's the Matter with Our Cat?

What's the matter with Thesaura, Mum?
What's the matter with our cat?
I know she's clever, but she's acting stranger
than ever, haven't you noticed that?

I know she's always on the table
sniffing among your books,
but now she's taken to flicking the pages
as if she's sneaking a look,

I know she likes your typewriter
but now she's pawing at the keys
and the way she curls her tail around it,
as if she has some trick up her sleeves.

She's acting more and more like a person,
don't laugh, Mum, it's true,
it's as if she's determined to be poetic
and show you that she can do it too.

# Spell to Make a Cat Word-struck

*Cattus Katta Kata*
*Kadis Katze Kazza*

Tail of mouse
and broom of stick
Whisker-bright
and full-moon trick
Creeping fur
and claw that prickle

Into the circle
words with a sizzle,
words be struck
and words be plucked
words be snatched
in a paw of luck

*Cattus Katta Kata*
*Kadis Katze Kazza*

## The Poet Cat

Our cat, Thesaura, is a poet
though she has no intention
of starving in a garret.

Like a poet she needs time
    to daydream
    and be keen
    to relax
    and be alert
To every sound-seeing
    on this earth.

Like a poet she is concerned
    most concerned
    with the stanzas
    of her fur
    and the licking
    into shape of her text
    and every pose
    she strikes
is in rhythm with herself.

Like a poet the pencils
of her nails are always
at the ready –
when inspiration strikes
she scratches out her lines
frantically.
> Be it upon
> the pad of a chair
> the page of a wall
> the papyrus of a tree
It's not her fault we can't read
> Cat-poetry.

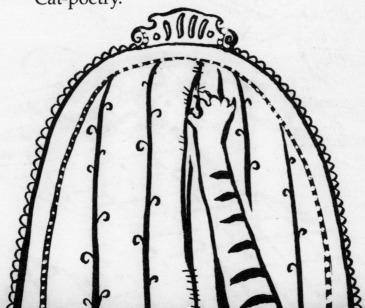

## Cat-Value

An alarm clock purring in the morning,
A furry hot-water bottle at night,
A torchlight with two little beams in the dark
                Value for money all right.

## Sleeping Out

What it is we cats get up to
when we don't come home?

What do we do? Where do we go?
Bet you humans would like to know.

Do we make a magic circle
recite poetry, dance and chortle?

Do we form an ancient pack
and prey along the railway track?

Do we set the night on fire
eyes emerald, sapphire?

Do we have a brawling, fur-flying,
caterwauling old knees-up?

Do we find a partner
and have a lovey-dovey smooch-up?

Or do I, bit-of-a-loner,
slink off under the warmth
of a parked car for shelter?

That's for me to know and you to wonder.

## Coming Up Roses

Don't think she's always
coming up roses.

With her humped back
and her snarl,
with her cat's leap
and her scrawl,
she too can be embroiled
in a brawl.
Slinking home after
with a patch of missing fur
and blood on her paws.

## Christmas Cheer

1

It wasn't as if I was asking for
gold, frankincense and myrrh,
none of these would have made me purr.
It would have been nice though
to sniff some little pressie for me
under that tree.

Still I will keep my cat-dignity

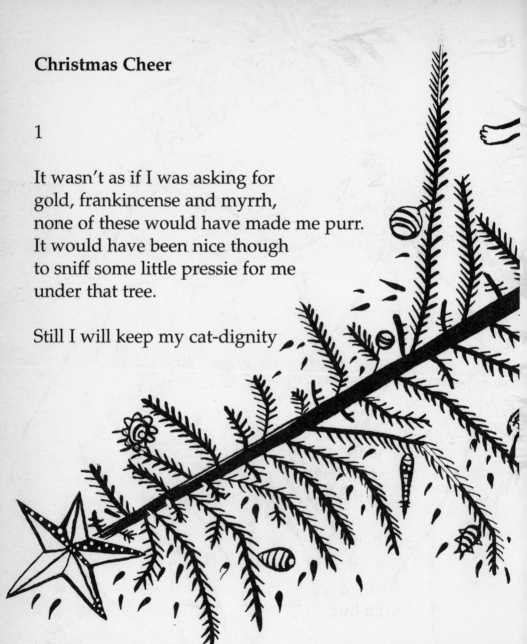

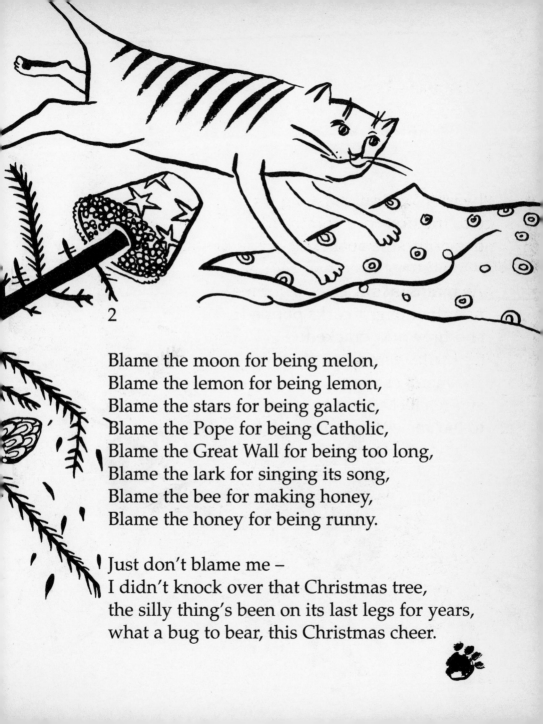

2

Blame the moon for being melon,
Blame the lemon for being lemon,
Blame the stars for being galactic,
Blame the Pope for being Catholic,
Blame the Great Wall for being too long,
Blame the lark for singing its song,
Blame the bee for making honey,
Blame the honey for being runny.

Just don't blame me –
I didn't knock over that Christmas tree,
the silly thing's been on its last legs for years,
what a bug to bear, this Christmas cheer.

## Millennium

I reckon our cat
was the first
to tap into the year 2000 –

As midnight struck
and champagne corks popped
and fireworks cracked

She merely sat up
and re-clocked her eyes
to the ancient timepiece of the sun.

## Alien in the Dark

She's an alien in the dark,
an extraterrestrial
looping across the park,

Eyes flying green saucers
coming over
the garden path

Come in, alien,
come in
from the dark

But what's this in your fur?
No stardust –
just a bit of bark and bur.

## Warden

Overlooking the garden
as if she's a warden,
treading on the daisies
without saying pardon,
circling the marigolds,
patting at a bee,
pretending indifference
to the birds on the tree.

# New Computer

Of course I was excited,
all that talk of a new computer
coming to the house with its own mouse!
I could hardly wait to greet it.

Until I saw it, bald as an egg,
plugged in by its tail to a socket.
I was cat-smacked.

Then I thought it must be in
some kind of hibernation mode
so I sniffed and waited, but could
smell nothing to stir my senses.

No squiggles,
no squeaks,
just clicks.

Then it hit me – it was plastic.
Didn't fool me for a minute.

## The Giving of Gifts

From time to time
I bring them gifts,
treasures that give my spirits
a definite lift –

A silvery glow-worm,
a small green sporty frog,
which I place carefully
on the backdoor mat,

But do these tokens
of cat-affection
receive any thanks or signs of pleasure?
No, just shriek-shriek-horror-horror,

And once again I see
my hard-earned trophies
being swept up and tossed
over the garden wall unceremoniously.

Forgive me then –
for feeling miffed
on this subject
of the giving of gifts.

## Why?

Why do people throw
shoes and things
whenever we cats decide
at nights to sing?

It's heart-rending,
their opposition,
to our musical compositions,
our varied renditions,

We have to listen
to their pop
and rock
and God knows what,

But whenever we cats
have a concert
they just seem
to go berserk,

Our moonlight sonatas
leave them cold,
no matter how much
we s-t-r-e-t-c-h our vocals,

But they are entitled
to their own opinions, humans,
to us our music is as beautiful
as Beethoven's or Schumann's.

## Cat-Dreaming

While we're hemmed in
by a blustery rain and wind,
she's trekking across hot desert sands,
stepping into ancient tombs
and cool magnificent temples,

She's witnessing first hand
what it means to be a mummy,
touching with her dreaming paw
the very place that boy-king Tutankhamun
lay with his bandaged tummy,

Now, having brushed past the pyramids
and the sphinx like a lynx,
she wakes up yawning widely at our boredom.
What a life, she has, our cat.
What a perfect-purrfect piece of a life.

## Nippy-Mothering

Every now and then
I give her a sudden nip,
half-playful
half-warning
furrily charming
and ultimately heart-warming,

But I can tell
she finds them disconcerting,
these sudden little nips
that seem to say, 'Pull your socks up quick.'
Dare she admit –
I am beginning to mother her a bit.

# Sekhmet

*Only the eyes of the cat*
*can outstare the serpent*
*Only the eyes of the cat*
*can outstare the serpent*

Ask Great Cat-Goddess Sekhmet,
headpiece, resplendent helmet,
as she guides the sun-barge each night
on its journey through the underworld.

Here, they must get past Great-Serpent,
the one they call, Fearsome Apep,
waiting in the cave of shadows
with his nightly threats of death.

But by the power of her cat's-eyes
she chills him through like malachite,
steering past his fixed fangs
of stalagmites and stalactites.

And once again Great Sekhmet hears
earth-people singing their hymns of praise
as they watch the sun-barge rising
with its golden promise of grain.

*Only the eyes of the cat*
*can outstare the serpent*
*Only the eyes of the cat*
*can outstare the serpent.*

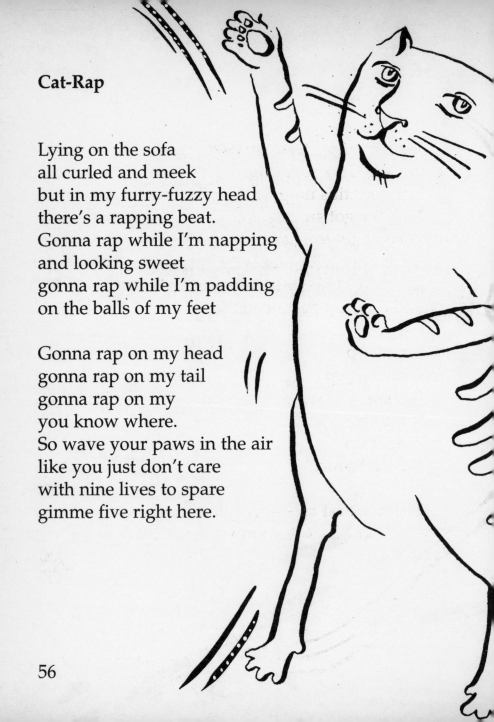

## Cat-Rap

Lying on the sofa
all curled and meek
but in my furry-fuzzy head
there's a rapping beat.
Gonna rap while I'm napping
and looking sweet
gonna rap while I'm padding
on the balls of my feet

Gonna rap on my head
gonna rap on my tail
gonna rap on my
you know where.
So wave your paws in the air
like you just don't care
with nine lives to spare
gimme five right here.

Well, they say that we cats
are killed by curiosity,
but does this moggie mind?
No, I've got suavity.
When I get to heaven
gonna rap with Macavity,
gonna find his hidden paw
and clear up that mystery.

Nap it up
scratch it up
the knack is free
fur it up
purr it up
yes that's me.

The meanest cat-rapper you'll ever see.
Number one of the street-sound galaxy.

## Weather Forecast

It will be raining cats.
Not cats and dogs,
just cats –
A dancing
twisting
spinning
whirling
down-pouring,
a furring out-pouring
from the grey
cushions of heaven.

58

It is advisable
to stay indoors,
or if you do go out
ensure a big brolly.

Off shore, on shore,
it will be raining cats
for sure.

This is the Cats' Weather Report.
It is the dogs' day off.

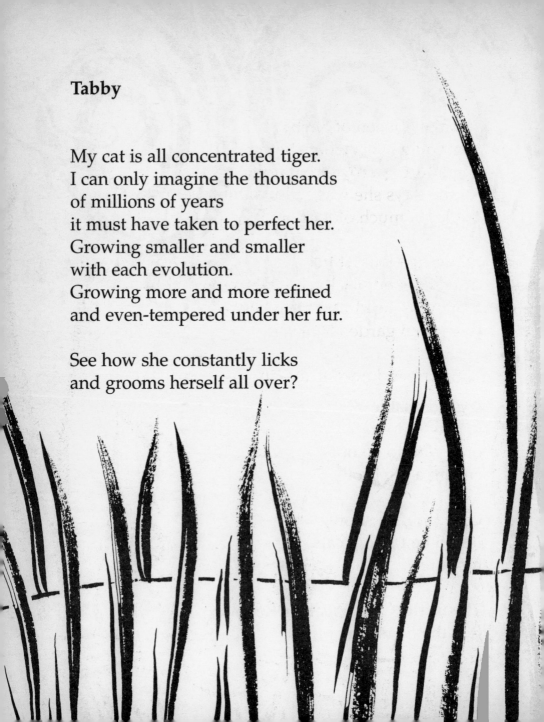

## Tabby

My cat is all concentrated tiger.
I can only imagine the thousands
of millions of years
it must have taken to perfect her.
Growing smaller and smaller
with each evolution.
Growing more and more refined
and even-tempered under her fur.

See how she constantly licks
and grooms herself all over?

A small Queen of Sheba
stamping everywhere her padded
signature – a royal reminder
of the days she was full-blown tiger.
Older O much older than Egypt.

Now, just look at her –
my grey and black tabby, stepping lightly,
emerging head first from between
the green garden stalks –

Ancient and new as the birth of a star.

## Coin

As earth as she's air –
a flash of hurricane
As velvet as she's fire –
a glowing stripy river

As blossom as she's thorn
surprises in a storm
As dark as she's light –
chatoyant-eyes in the night

A two-sided coin
if ever there was one.

## A note on Sekhmet and Tutankhamun

*Sekhmet* - Egyptian Lion-headed Goddess and guardian of the boat of the Sun God on its journey through the underworld. In her fiercest form she is the noontime Sun, intense and blinding.

*Tutankhamun* - Famous Egyptian boy-king whose tomb still exists in the Valley of the Kings where the tombs of many pharaohs still lie. His body was wrapped in linen and over his face was placed a golden mask. Over 3000 treasures were found in his tomb.